★ *A Daily Journal of Gratitude & Love* ★

# NICK KEOMAHAVONG

# DEDICATION

*This journal is dedicated to all who have selflessly provided support, inspiration, and unconditional love.*

# ★ PERSONAL MESSAGE ★

TO:
FROM:

Date:___________________          Day #___________________

# I LOVE YOU BECAUSE...

_______________________________________________

_______________________________________________

_______________________________________________

_______________________________________________

_______________________________________________

_______________________________________________

_______________________________________________

_______________________________________________

_______________________________________________

_______________________________________________

_______________________________________________

_______________________________________________

_______________________________________________

*Draw the feeling...*

Date:_______________        Day #___________

# I LOVE YOU BECAUSE...

Date:_________________     Day #___________

# I LOVE YOU BECAUSE...

Date:________________  Day #__________

# I LOVE YOU BECAUSE...

Date:_________________          Day #_____________

# I LOVE YOU BECAUSE...

Date:_______________     Day #__________

# I LOVE YOU BECAUSE...

Date:________________    Day #____________

# I LOVE YOU BECAUSE...

# I LOVE YOU BECAUSE...

Date:___________________     Day #___________________

# I LOVE YOU BECAUSE...

Date:_____________________ Day #_____________________

# I LOVE YOU BECAUSE...

Date:______________________    Day #____________

# I LOVE YOU BECAUSE...

Date:________________          Day #__________

# I LOVE YOU BECAUSE...

Date:__________________     Day #__________________

# I LOVE YOU BECAUSE...

_______________________________________________

_______________________________________________

_______________________________________________

_______________________________________________

_______________________________________________

_______________________________________________

_______________________________________________

_______________________________________________

_______________________________________________

_______________________________________________

_______________________________________________

Date:_________________          Day #________

# I LOVE YOU BECAUSE...

Date:_______________ Day #_________

# I LOVE YOU BECAUSE...

Date:_________________ Day #__________

# I LOVE YOU BECAUSE... 

___________________________________________
___________________________________________
___________________________________________
___________________________________________
___________________________________________
___________________________________________
___________________________________________
___________________________________________
___________________________________________
___________________________________________
___________________________________________
___________________________________________

Date:_______________     Day #__________

# I LOVE YOU BECAUSE...

Date:________________     Day #__________

# I LOVE YOU BECAUSE...

Date:_________________     Day #_____________

# I LOVE YOU BECAUSE...

Date:_________________        Day #_____________

# I LOVE YOU BECAUSE...

Date:_______________     Day #__________

# I LOVE YOU BECAUSE...

Date:_________________     Day #_____________

# I LOVE YOU BECAUSE...

Date:_________________     Day #_________________

# I LOVE YOU BECAUSE...

Date:_______________     Day #_______________

# I LOVE YOU BECAUSE...

Date:________________  Day #__________

# I LOVE YOU BECAUSE...

Date:_________________        Day #_____________

# I LOVE YOU BECAUSE...

Date:_______________        Day #_________

# I LOVE YOU BECAUSE...

Date:_________________   Day #_____________

# I LOVE YOU BECAUSE...

Date:_______________    Day #___________

# I LOVE YOU BECAUSE...

Date:____________________     Day #_____________

# I LOVE YOU BECAUSE...

Date:_________________      Day #_________________

# I LOVE YOU BECAUSE...

_________________________________________

_________________________________________

_________________________________________

_________________________________________

_________________________________________

_________________________________________

_________________________________________

_________________________________________

_________________________________________

_________________________________________

_________________________________________

_________________________________________

_________________________________________

_________________________________________

_________________________________________

Date:________________        Day #______________

# I LOVE YOU BECAUSE...

Date:_______________        Day #_______________

# I LOVE YOU BECAUSE...

Date:_________________          Day #_____________

# I LOVE YOU BECAUSE...

Date:_________________     Day #__________________

# I LOVE YOU BECAUSE...

Date:_________________ Day #___________

# I LOVE YOU BECAUSE...

Date:__________________     Day #__________________

# I LOVE YOU BECAUSE...

Date:_________________        Day #_____________

# I LOVE YOU BECAUSE...

Date:_________________        Day #___________

# I LOVE YOU BECAUSE...

Date:_______________     Day #_______________

# I LOVE YOU BECAUSE...

Date:_________________________     Day #____________________

# I LOVE YOU BECAUSE...

________________________________________________

________________________________________________

________________________________________________

________________________________________________

________________________________________________

________________________________________________

________________________________________________

________________________________________________

________________________________________________

________________________________________________

________________________________________________

________________________________________________

________________________________________________

Date:_________________          Day #_________________

# I LOVE YOU BECAUSE...

Date:_______________     Day #_____________

# I LOVE YOU BECAUSE...

Date:__________________    Day #__________________

# I LOVE YOU BECAUSE...

Date:_______________     Day #___________

# I LOVE YOU BECAUSE...

Date:________________          Day #________________

# I LOVE YOU BECAUSE...

Date:_________________________     Day #_________________________

# I LOVE YOU BECAUSE...

Date:_______________     Day #_______________

# I LOVE YOU BECAUSE...

Date:________________    Day #__________

# I LOVE YOU BECAUSE...

_______________________________________

_______________________________________

_______________________________________

_______________________________________

_______________________________________

_______________________________________

_______________________________________

_______________________________________

_______________________________________

_______________________________________

_______________________________________

_______________________________________

_______________________________________

Date:_____________________     Day #_____________

# I LOVE YOU BECAUSE...

Date:________________        Day #__________

# I LOVE YOU BECAUSE...

Date:_________________          Day #_____________

# I LOVE YOU BECAUSE...

Date:_______________          Day #_____________

# I LOVE YOU BECAUSE...

Date:_________________          Day #___________

# I LOVE YOU BECAUSE...

Date:_______________     Day #_______________

# I LOVE YOU BECAUSE...

Date:_______________          Day #___________

# I LOVE YOU BECAUSE...

Date:_____________________     Day #__________

# I LOVE YOU BECAUSE...

Date:_______________     Day #_________

# I LOVE YOU BECAUSE...

Date:_______________          Day #___________

# I LOVE YOU BECAUSE...

Date:_______________          Day #__________

# I LOVE YOU BECAUSE...

Date:________________    Day #________

# I LOVE YOU BECAUSE...

Date:_________________ Day #_____________

# I LOVE YOU BECAUSE...

Date:_______________          Day #___________

# I LOVE YOU BECAUSE...

Date:_________________       Day #_____________

# I LOVE YOU BECAUSE...

# I LOVE YOU BECAUSE...

Date:_________________     Day #_____________

# I LOVE YOU BECAUSE...

Date:___________          Day #__________

I LOVE YOU BECAUSE...

Draw the feeling...

Date:_________________     Day #_____________

# I LOVE YOU BECAUSE...

Date:_________________        Day #_________

# I LOVE YOU BECAUSE...

Date:________________    Day #__________

# I LOVE YOU BECAUSE...

Date:_______________          Day #_____________

# I LOVE YOU BECAUSE...

Date:_______________          Day #_____________

# I LOVE YOU BECAUSE...

Date:_______________________  Day #_____________

# I LOVE YOU BECAUSE...

Date:_____________     Day #_____________

# I LOVE YOU BECAUSE...

Date:_________________   Day #_____________

# I LOVE YOU BECAUSE...

Date:_______________ Day #_______________

# I LOVE YOU BECAUSE...

Date:_________________        Day #__________

# I LOVE YOU BECAUSE...

Date:_______________     Day #_____________

# I LOVE YOU BECAUSE...

# I LOVE YOU BECAUSE...

Date:_______________     Day #_____________

# I LOVE YOU BECAUSE...

Date:_______________    Day #__________

# I LOVE YOU BECAUSE...

Date:_______________          Day #_____________

# I LOVE YOU BECAUSE...

Date:_______________  Day #___________

# I LOVE YOU BECAUSE...

Date:_______________        Day #_______________

# I LOVE YOU BECAUSE...

Date:_________________      Day #_____________

# I LOVE YOU BECAUSE...

Date:_______________     Day #___________

# I LOVE YOU BECAUSE...

Date:_________________    Day #___________

# I LOVE YOU BECAUSE...

Date:_________________          Day #_________________

# I LOVE YOU BECAUSE...

Date:________________    Day #__________

# I LOVE YOU BECAUSE...

Date:_________________     Day #_____________

# I LOVE YOU BECAUSE...

Date:__________________        Day #__________________

# I LOVE YOU BECAUSE...

Date:________________          Day #____________

# I LOVE YOU BECAUSE...

Date:_________________     Day #_____________

# I LOVE YOU BECAUSE...

Date:_______________          Day #__________

# I LOVE YOU BECAUSE...

Date:_________________          Day #_____________

# I LOVE YOU BECAUSE...

Date:___________________     Day #___________________

# I LOVE YOU BECAUSE...

www.ingramcontent.com/pod-product-compliance
Lightning Source LLC
Chambersburg PA
CBHW050036260726